SANTOI

TRAVEL

GUIDE

The Ultimate Guide to A Journey Through the Attractions, Food, Wine, and Culture on Greece's Island. Everything You Need to Know Before Planning a Trip to Santorini

ANTHONY TURNER

TABLE OF CONTENT

INTRODUCTION

Santorini is a place that has left a memorable impression on me. I was captivated by the beauty of the terrain and the warmth of the people the moment I arrived on the island. Every day provided fresh events and memories that I will treasure for the rest of my life.

Visiting the village of Oia was one of the most memorable parts of my trip. The white-washed buildings perched on the caldera's edge were gorgeous, and the sunset over the Aegean Sea was simply breathtaking. It was as if I were living in a postcard.

Another highlight of my vacation was visiting Akrotiri, an old Minoan site. The excavations revealed a complex and thriving civilisation that existed thousands of years ago, and I was awestruck by the amount of preservation and depth of history that I was experiencing.

But it was the people that made my trip to Santorini genuinely memorable. I was greeted with warmth and hospitality everywhere I went. I felt like I was among friends, whether it was a local shopkeeper who shared their family's fava recipe or a tour guide who regaled me with anecdotes about the island's history.

I recall eating at a taverna in Pyrgos village. While I was eating, the owner of the taverna approached me to chat. We ended up discussing everything from Santorini's history to our favorite books for hours. It was a genuine moment of bonding that I will never forget.

When I think back on my time in Santorini, I'm filled with appreciation for the experiences I had and the people I met. It's a place I'd suggest to anyone looking for beauty, history, and spiritual warmth. If you have the opportunity to visit Santorini, take advantage of it. You will not be disappointed!

About Santorini

Santorini is a Greek island in the Aegean Sea that forms part of the Cyclades archipelago. It is well-known for its breathtaking beauty, distinctive volcanic landscape, and rich history. The island is famous for its unique white-washed homes with blue domes standing on cliff edges overlooking the caldera, a vast volcanic crater formed thousands of years ago.

Santorini has a remarkable history that dates back thousands of years. The Minoans, one of the world's most advanced civilizations, lived on the island. One of Greece's most important archaeological sites is Akrotiri, which was buried by a volcanic explosion in 1627 BC.

Santorini is becoming a major tourist destination, drawing visitors from all over the world. The island is well-known for its lovely beaches, pristine oceans, and breathtaking sunsets. Visitors can stroll around the lovely towns, savor the delectable local cuisine, and try some of the island's famed wines.

Santorini's volcanic terrain, which has influenced the island's topography and history, is one of its most distinguishing aspects. The island's still-active volcano has left its mark on the landscape, forming stunning cliffs, rocky terrain, and unusual rock formations.

Santorini has something for everyone, whether you're looking for relaxation, adventure, culture, or a little bit of everything. With its spectacular beauty, rich history, kind friendliness, and delectable cuisine, it's no surprise that Santorini is one of Greece's most popular tourist destinations.

Why Visit Santorini

There are numerous reasons why you should visit Santorini; it certainly has something for everyone. Here are a few more reasons why Santorini should be at the top of your travel wish list:

Breathtaking Views: Santorini is famous for its breathtaking views of the caldera and the Aegean Sea. The classic white-washed buildings standing on the cliff's edge provide an unrivaled perspective that is simply unforgettable.

Rich History: Santorini has a rich history, dating back to the ancient Minoan civilization and continuing through the Byzantine and Venetian centuries. Visitors can learn about the island's history by visiting intriguing archaeological sites and museums.

Beautiful Beaches: Santorini is well-known for its spectacular cliffside vistas, but it also has some of Greece's most beautiful beaches. There is something for every type of beach enthusiast, from famous black sand beaches to secret coves and isolated bays.

Delicious Cuisine and Wine: Santorini is famed for its distinct culinary traditions, with dishes that feature fresh seafood, local produce, and traditional ingredients. No vacation to Santorini would be complete without drinking some of the island's famous wines, which are crafted from indigenous grape varietals.

Warm Hospitality: The people of Santorini are noted for their friendly spirit and warm hospitality. You'll feel completely at home, whether you're conversing with a local shopkeeper, dining at a traditional taverna, or exploring the island with a knowledgeable guide.

In short, Santorini provides a balance of beauty, history, culture, gastronomy, and spiritual warmth. It's a place that every traveler should consider, whether they're looking for pleasure, adventure, or a little of both. So, why should you go to Santorini? Why wouldn't you, is the actual question.

A Brief Overview of the Island's History and Culture

Santorini has a long and illustrious history and culture dating back thousands of years. The island has been inhabited since prehistoric times and was home to one of the ancient world's most advanced civilizations, the Minoans.

The Minoans were recognized for their complex culture, art, and architecture and resided on the island around 2000 BC. Akrotiri, the ancient city buried by a volcanic eruption in 1627 BC, is a witness to their great culture. The ruins of the city, unearthed in the 1960s, offer an intriguing peek into Minoan life.

For many years following the volcanic explosion, the island was deserted. It was afterward settled by the Phoenicians, who were followed by the Greeks, who founded Thira in the 9th century BC. The island grew to be an important trading and commercial center in the Aegean.

Santorini was influential during the Byzantine and Venetian eras, and the island's architecture and culture reflect this. The Ottoman Empire later conquered the island, followed by the Germans during World War II.

Santorini is currently a renowned tourist destination noted for its magnificent beauty, rich history, and distinct culture. The architecture of the island, which has white-washed buildings with blue domes, is a symbol of Greece. The cuisine on the island is likewise a distinct blend of traditional Greek and Mediterranean cuisines, with a focus on fresh seafood and local products.

The people of Santorini are known for their great hospitality and welcoming spirit. Visitors to the island can immerse themselves in traditional Greek culture through music, dance, and festivals held throughout the year. Overall, Santorini's history and culture are a fascinating blend of ancient and modern influences, making the island a genuinely one-of-a-kind and memorable destination.

CHAPTER 1:
PLANNING YOUR TRIP TO SANTORINI

Santorini is one of Greece's most popular tourist destinations. The island is well-known for its breathtaking beauty, rich history, and distinct culture, making it a great vacation destination for people of all ages and interests.

Planning a trip to Santorini, on the other hand, might be daunting, especially if you're unfamiliar with the island. This chapter is intended to assist you in planning your trip to Santorini so that you can make the most of your vacation and create amazing memories.

In this chapter, we'll go over everything you need to know to plan your vacation to Santorini, from when to go to where to stay to how to travel around the island. You'll also get advice on what to pack and how to get ready for your trip.

Planning a trip to Santorini, whether you're a first-time visitor or a seasoned tourist, can be very challenging.

However, with the correct information and resources, you can make the most of your stay on the island and enjoy everything it has to offer.

So, let's get started on arranging your trip to Santorini and turning your vacation dreams into reality. Santorini will steal your heart and leave you wanting more, from the spectacular caldera vistas to the lovely villages and beaches.

When to Go

When planning a trip to Santorini, consider the optimum time to visit to make the most of your vacation. The temperature, seasonal events, and tourist throngs on the island might all influence your decision.

Santorini's peak tourist season lasts from mid-June to early September. The island can be highly congested during this season, and prices for lodgings, activities, and restaurants may be higher than at other times of the year. The weather, on the other hand, is often warm and bright, making it ideal for swimming and sunbathing.

Consider visiting Santorini during the shoulder seasons of April to June or September to November for a quieter and more economical vacation. The weather is still beautiful throughout these months, and the crowds are lower. Furthermore, many restaurants and attractions provide off-season discounts.

Winter is Santorini's low season, and while the island might be cold and rainy during this time, there is still enough to do and see. You can experience the island's rich cultural past, explore local vineyards, or participate in one-of-a-kind winter activities like the Carnival celebrations.

Overall, the best time to visit Santorini is determined by your tastes and travel style. Santorini has something for everyone, whether you want a calm beach vacation or a cultural excursion.

How to Get to Santorini

Depending on your location and travel preferences, you can reach Santorini via airline, boat, or cruise ship.

By Plane: Santorini has its airport, Santorini (Thira) National Airport, located near Kamari village. During the peak tourist season, many airlines operate daily flights to and from Santorini, with fewer flights available during the offseason. Connecting flights are also available from Athens and other major Greek cities.

By Ferry: If you want a more picturesque and cost-effective option, riding a ferry to Santorini may be the way to go. The island has two main ports, Athinios and the old port of Fira, both of which are supplied by ferries from Athens and other Aegean Sea islands. The ferry travel time varies based on your location and the type of vessel, with some routes taking as little as two hours and others taking up to eight hours.

By Cruise Ship: Santorini is a popular stop for many cruise ships, which dock at Athinios port. If you arrive by cruise ship, you can take a guided tour or explore the island on your own, utilizing public transit or a cab.

Whatever mode of transportation you pick to get to Santorini, make sure to book it in advance to confirm availability and avoid any last-minute travel issues.

Getting Around Santorini

Getting around Santorini is simple, and there are numerous transportation alternatives to suit your budget and interests.

Public Transportation: The island offers a dependable and reasonably priced public transportation system comprised of buses that run between the main towns and villages. The buses are air-conditioned and have comfy seats, making them an easy way to get around the island. Tickets can be purchased aboard or at bus terminals at cheap prices.

Taxis: Taxis are an alternative mode of transportation in Santorini, however, they are more expensive than public transportation. Taxis are easily accessible at the airport, ports, and major cities, and can be summoned on the street or by phone. It should be noted that taxi charges can vary depending on the time of day and distance traveled.

Rental Cars and Scooters: Renting a car or scooter can be a terrific alternative if you desire more independence and flexibility in your travels. There are various rental agencies located throughout the island, with pricing varying based on the type of car and the length of the rental time. Driving in Santorini can be difficult due to the small roads, steep hills, and heavy traffic during the peak tourist season.

Walking: Many of Santorini's attractions, like its picturesque villages, beaches, and archaeological monuments, are accessible by foot. Walking is a terrific way to experience the scenic splendor of the island and immerse yourself in its culture.

Whatever mode of transportation you select to travel around Santorini, it's critical to plan and evaluates the most efficient and cost-effective alternative for your needs. Santorini, with its magnificent landscapes and rich cultural past, is best explored at your speed.

Where to Stay in Santorini

From luxury hotels and villas to budget-friendly guesthouses and hostels, Santorini has a wide choice of lodging options to suit all budgets and preferences.

Oia: Oia is a popular and scenic settlement on the island, famed for its breathtaking sunsets, blue-domed churches, and quaint small alleyways. Accommodation options in the village range from fancy cave hotels to traditional guesthouses.

Fira: Fira is the capital and largest town on the island, located on the west coast. The town is a retail, culinary, and nightlife hotspot, as well as a historic site, the Archaeological Museum of Thera. Fira's lodging options range from low-cost hostels to expensive hotels and resorts.

Imerovigli: Located between Fira and Oia, Imerovigli is a tranquil and charming village with amazing views of the caldera and the Aegean Sea. The village is home to several luxury hotels and villas, making it a great location for honeymooners and couples.

Kamari: Kamari is a prominent beach resort on Santorini's southeast coast, famed for its black sand beach and boisterous atmosphere. Accommodation options in the area range from budget-friendly guesthouses to luxury hotels and resorts.

Whatever hotel you choose to stay in Santorini, make sure to book well in advance, especially during the peak tourist season. Santorini is a destination that visitors will remember for its breathtaking landscapes, vibrant culture, and kind hospitality.

Choosing the Right Accommodation in Santorini

Choosing the right Santorini accommodation may make or break your vacation experience. Here are some of the various types of accommodations on the island to help you choose the best one for your needs:

Luxury Hotels: Santorini is home to some of the world's most magnificent hotels, with stunning caldera views, private plunge pools, and spa services. Canaves Oia Suites, Grace Santorini, and Andronis Luxury Suites are a few examples of luxury hotels on the island.

Villas: If you're traveling with a group or want a more private and intimate experience, renting a villa can be an excellent choice. Santorini offers a wide range of homes, from classic cave houses to modern villas with private pools. Santorini Princess Presidential Suites, Villa Dakoronia, and Villa Fabrica are some examples of villa rentals on the island.

Budget Accommodations: If you're traveling on a tight budget, Santorini boasts several budget-friendly lodging options. Hostels, guesthouses, and apartments on the island can offer a comfortable and reasonable stay. Villa Manos, Markakis Studios, and Anny Studios Perissa are some examples of low-cost accommodations on the island.

Traditional Cave Houses: One of Santorini's distinguishing features is its traditional cave houses, which are cut into the island's volcanic cliffs. These houses provide a traditional and authentic experience, with many giving breathtaking caldera views. Caveland, Aris Caves, and Nikos Villas are some examples of classic cave dwellings on the island.

Whatever sort of lodging you pick, make sure to book ahead of time, especially during high tourist season, to assure availability and the best pricing. Santorini, with its magnificent scenery, kind hospitality, and rich culture, is a location that will leave you with memories to last a lifetime.

What to Pack

Packing for a trip to Santorini can be difficult because the weather and activities on the island fluctuate depending on the time of year you visit. Here are some must-have products for your Santorini vacation:

Comfortable Clothing: Lightweight, breathable clothes that are suitable to wear in warm weather should be packed. Shorts, tees, sundresses, and swimsuits are all excellent choices.

Sun Protection: Because Santorini is known for its sunny weather, bring plenty of sunscreens, sunglasses, and a hat to protect your skin from the sun's harsh rays.

Walking Shoes: You'll most likely be strolling about the island, so bring comfortable, supportive shoes. Sandals or sneakers are both suitable options.

A Camera: Because Santorini is one of the most beautiful places in the world, you'll want to record all of the breathtaking vistas and memories.

A Day Bag: A lightweight day bag is crucial for transporting everyday necessities like water, food, sunscreen, and your camera.

Swimwear: There are several gorgeous beaches in Santorini, so bring your favorite swimsuit.

Light Jacket: Evenings on the island can be cool, especially during the shoulder season, so bring a lightweight jacket or sweater for cooler nights.

Power Adapters: Because Santorini uses European electrical outlets, carry power adapters for any electronic gadgets you intend to bring.

Packing these necessary goods will ensure that you are prepared for all of the activities and weather that Santorini has to offer. Pack light and leave extra room in your luggage for souvenirs and treasures you'll find on the island.

Entry and Visa Requirements

Santorini has the same entry requirements as Greece. You do not require a visa to visit Santorini or Greece if you are a citizen of the European Union (EU) or the European Economic Area (EEA). On arrival, all you'll need is a valid passport or national ID card.

If you are a citizen of a country other than the EU/EEA, you may be required to obtain a visa to enter Greece. Visa requirements differ depending on your country of origin, the purpose and length of your travel, and other variables.

You can check the visa requirements for your country on the Greek Ministry of Foreign Affairs official website, or you can contact your nearest Greek embassy or consulate. If you require a visa, make your application well in advance of your trip to allow for processing time.

It's also worth noting that, during the COVID-19 pandemic, Greece imposed travel restrictions and health procedures.

Before planning a trip to Santorini, make sure to check the Greek National Tourism Organization's official website for the most up-to-date travel advisories and entrance requirements.

Currency and Language

Santorini, like the rest of Greece, uses the Euro (EUR) as its currency. Foreign currency can be exchanged in banks, exchange offices, and some hotels, but it's a good idea to compare exchange rates and costs before proceeding.

The official language of Santorini and Greece is Greek, however many inhabitants, particularly in tourist areas, also speak English. You shouldn't have any trouble communicating with locals or getting around, but knowing a few basic Greek phrases like "hello" (o, pronounced "yia sou"), "thank you" (, pronounced "efharisto"), and "goodbye" (, pronounced "adio") can go a long way toward demonstrating your respect and appreciation for the local culture.

Suggested Budget

Santorini is known for its opulent and upscale atmosphere, yet the island can still be visited on a budget. Your budget will be determined by several things, including the time of year you visit, your travel style, and the activities you intend to participate in. Here is a breakdown of some typical expenses in Santorini:

Accommodations: Accommodations in Santorini range in price from low-cost guesthouses and hostels to high-end resorts and villas. Depending on the sort of hotel, expect to pay between €30 and €500 per night.

Food and Drink: Santorini offers a variety of dining alternatives, ranging from traditional Greek tavernas to high-end restaurants serving gourmet cuisines. A meal at a mid-range restaurant should cost between €10 and €25, and a beer or glass of wine should cost between €3 and €5.

Transportation: The island has public transportation, with buses traveling between the main towns and settlements. A one-way bus ticket costs between €2 and €3. Taxis are also available, however, they can be costly. With prices starting at about €25 per day, renting a car or scooter can be a simple and cost-effective way to move around.

Activities: Santorini has a wide range of activities, from hiking and beach hopping to wine tasting and boat trips. Some activities are free, such as hiking or exploring the island's beaches, while others, such as boat tours or wine tastings, might cost anywhere from €20 to €100+ per person.

Overall, depending on your travel style and tastes, you should anticipate spending between €50 and €200 each day in Santorini. Santorini's beauty and charm may be experienced without breaking the bank with smart preparation and budgeting.

Money-Saving Tips

Regardless of Santorini's luxurious lifestyle, there are ways to conserve money while still enjoying everything the island has to offer. Here are some money-saving strategies to help you stretch your Santorini budget:

Visit during the shoulder season: When compared to the high season (June-August), prices for lodgings, meals, and activities are often lower during the shoulder season (April-May and September-October).

Stay in budget-friendly accommodation: You don't have to stay in a high-end resort or villa to enjoy Santorini. To save money on lodging, consider staying at a guesthouse or hostel.

Use public transportation: Buses are an easy and inexpensive way to move about the island. A one-way bus ticket costs between €2-€3, whereas a taxi ride can cost significantly more.

Cook your meals: Because many Santorini accommodations have kitchens, you can save money by making your own meals instead of eating out every meal.

Explore the island on foot: There are several wonderful hiking trails and walking pathways on Santorini that are free to use and give stunning views of the island.

Visit free attractions: Santorini has several free attractions, such as beaches and museums, that you may enjoy without spending any money.

Book activities in advance: Booking activities in advance, such as boat tours and wine tastings, can often save you money over booking on the spot.

You can enjoy the beauty and charm of Santorini without breaking the bank if you follow these money-saving recommendations.

Best Places to Book Your Trip

You can book your trip to Santorini using a variety of online travel agents and booking sites. Here are some of the best places to book your trip:

Booking.com: From budget-friendly guesthouses to high-end villas, Booking.com has a wide choice of accommodations in Santorini. You can also narrow down your search by price, location, and amenities.

Airbnb: For those looking for unique and local accommodations in Santorini, Airbnb is a popular option. Everything from a solitary room to a whole villa or apartment can be rented.

Expedia: Expedia offers a range of Santorini holiday packages that include flights, lodging, and activities. You may also book vehicle rentals and transfers through the website.

Kayak: Kayak is a travel search engine that lets you compare the costs of flights, hotels, and rental vehicles. You can also use the site to set price alerts and monitor price changes over time.

Tripadvisor: Tripadvisor is a prominent travel review site that also allows you to book Santorini lodgings, flights, and activities. The site includes reviews and ratings from other travelers, which can assist you in making an informed selection when planning your vacation.

If you book your trip somewhere, make sure to check reviews and compare prices to verify you're receiving the best bargain.

CHAPTER 2:
EXPLORING SANTORINI'S TOWNS AND VILLAGES

Exploring Santorini's towns and villages is a must-do for any visitor to this gorgeous island. Each town and village has its distinct personality, giving tourists a taste of Santorini's rich history, culture, and natural beauty. Santorini's towns and villages are a feast for the senses, from the distinctive white-washed structures perched on the cliffs to the lively streets crowded with stores and restaurants.

In this chapter, we'll look at some of Santorini's most popular cities and villages, including Fira, Oia, and Akrotiri. We'll look at their history, culture, and prominent attractions, as well as offer advice on how to get around and enjoy each town or hamlet.

Santorini's towns and villages have something for everyone, whether you want to shop for souvenirs, taste wonderful local cuisine, or simply take in the spectacular vistas.

So are you ready to explore the charming streets and hidden corners of Santorini's towns and villages, discovering the beauty that has enchanted visitors for years? Let's go!

Oia: The Iconic Village on the Edge of the Caldera

Oia, perched on the rim of the caldera, is undoubtedly Santorini's most iconic and gorgeous settlement. Oia, with its white-washed homes, blue-domed churches, and winding lanes, provides visitors with a picture of traditional Greek island life.

Oia's history dates back to the 13th century when Venetian conquerors established the village on the site of an earlier Minoan settlement. Oia became a trading and business hub over the centuries, with sailors and merchants from all over the world passing through its port. Oia is currently well-known for its art galleries, boutique stores, and thriving cultural community.

Top Attractions:
The famed sunset view, which draws throngs of visitors every evening, is one of Oia's main attractions. From one of the many rooftop pubs and restaurants, or the cliffside castle ruins, you can watch the sun set below the horizon. The Maritime Museum, which documents the island's

seafaring history, and the Byzantine Castle Ruins, which offer breathtaking views of the village and the caldera, are also famous attractions in Oia.

Getting Around:
Oia is a pedestrian-friendly community, with most streets and alleyways accessible only on foot. Expect steep climbs and small walkways, but the breathtaking views and gorgeous architecture make it all worthwhile. You can also rent an ATV or scooter to explore the nearby area if you're feeling adventurous.

Where to Stay:
Oia has some of Santorini's most luxurious and romantic lodgings, including high-end hotels and private villas. However, there are more affordable options, such as guesthouses and flats, in the hamlet and surrounding area.

Dining & Nightlife:
Oia is well-known for its luxury dining options, with several restaurants offering gourmet cuisine and spectacular caldera views. Head to one of the traditional tavernas or cafes for local Greek delicacies for a more informal

experience. Oia also boasts a lively nightlife, with various bars and clubs featuring live music and dancing.

Oia is a must-see location in Santorini, whether you want to soak up the sun, immerse yourself in history and culture, or simply enjoy the breathtaking vistas.

Fira: The Bustling Capital of Santorini

Fira is Santorini's bustling center and a popular destination for travelers from all over the world. Fira is a must-see location on any trip to Santorini, with its meandering alleyways, busy nightlife, and spectacular views of the caldera.

History and Culture:
Fira has a long and illustrious history reaching back to the prehistoric age. The ancient ruins, including the Agora marketplace and the Archaeological Museum of Thera, demonstrate the town's rich cultural legacy. Fira also has several antique churches and cathedrals, including the magnificent Orthodox Cathedral of Saint John the Baptist.

Top Attractions:
The cable car trip that carries visitors from the old harbor up to the town is one of Fira's major attractions. The ride provides stunning views of the caldera and the Aegean Sea. Other famous Fira attractions include the Museum of Prehistoric Thera, which displays items from the island's

ancient past, and the lively center square, where visitors may soak in the local culture.

Getting Around:
Fira is a pedestrian-friendly town, with most streets and alleyways only accessible on foot. However, taxis and buses are available to transport guests to other sections of the island.

Where to Stay:
Fira has lodgings for every price, ranging from luxury hotels to budget-friendly guesthouses and hostels. The town's central location makes it an ideal starting point for visiting the rest of the island.

Dining and Nightlife:
Fira has a thriving dining and nightlife scene. There are various fancy restaurants and pubs in town, as well as traditional tavernas providing traditional Greek cuisine. Visitors can also enjoy live music and dancing in the town center's numerous clubs and pubs.

Fira is a must-see location on any trip to Santorini, whether you're interested in history and culture, shopping and dining, or simply taking in the breathtaking vistas.

Akrotiri: The Minoan Site and Archaeological Wonder

Akrotiri is a small village on Santorini's southwestern edge, famous for its spectacular Minoan archaeological site and unusual geological formations. Visitors go to Akrotiri to explore the ancient ruins and learn about the intriguing history of the island.

History and Culture:
The archaeological site of Akrotiri is one of the most significant prehistoric settlements in the Aegean. The site was found in 1967 and has since been intensively excavated, revealing a sophisticated and complex Bronze Age society. The well-preserved ruins, which include multi-story houses, paved streets, and elaborate paintings showing scenes from everyday life, can be explored by visitors.

Top Attractions:
Akrotiri is recognized for its remarkable geological formations in addition to its historic site. With its characteristic red and black volcanic sand and high cliffs, Red Beach is a famous tourist destination. The neighboring

White Beach provides a more private and peaceful setting, ideal for a relaxed day by the sea.

Getting Around:
Akrotiri is easily accessible from other sections of the island by bus or automobile. Visitors can also take advantage of a guided tour of the archaeological site to learn more about its history and significance.

Where to Stay:
While Akrotiri has few housing options, guests can stay in neighboring towns such as Perissa or Kamari, which have a variety of hotels, guesthouses, and villas.

Dining and Nightlife:
Akrotiri is a sleepy village with few alternatives for dining and entertainment. Nearby towns like Fira and Oia, on the other hand, have a variety of restaurants and taverns serving both local and foreign cuisine.

Akrotiri is a must-see site on every trip to Santorini, whether you're a history buff, a nature lover, or simply looking for a calm vacation.

Pyrgos: The Picturesque Hilltop Village

Pyrgos is a lovely hilltop village in Santorini's center, famed for its attractive streets, breathtaking views, and classic Cycladic buildings. Pyrgos visitors can expect to be taken back in time, surrounded by centuries-old buildings and a calm, relaxed ambience.

History and Culture:
Pyrgos was originally the capital of Santorini and is steeped in history and culture. Visitors can visit the ruins of a Venetian castle from the 15th century, as well as the exquisite churches and chapels scattered throughout the village. The tiny, meandering alleyways and whitewashed buildings showcase ancient Cycladic architecture, while the breathtaking views of the surrounding landscape and sea convey a sense of tranquility and serenity.

Top Attractions:
In addition to historical and cultural attractions, Pyrgos is noted for its breathtaking panoramic vistas. Climb to the top of the village for panoramic views of the island and the

Aegean Sea. The village also has a variety of stores and restaurants, making it ideal for a stroll or a calm supper.

Getting Around:

Pyrgos is easily accessible from other sections of the island by bus or automobile. Visitors can also choose to walk around the village, soaking in the sights and sounds of this delightful hilltop town.

Where to Stay:

Pyrgos has a variety of lodging alternatives, including traditional guesthouses and luxurious villas. Visitors can stay in the town center, surrounded by attractive streets and buildings, or in the surrounding countryside, which offers a more calm and private ambiance.

Dining and Nightlife:

Pyrgos has a variety of dining options, ranging from traditional tavernas providing traditional Greek cuisine to upmarket restaurants serving foreign cuisine. Visitors can also enjoy a drink or two at one of the village's numerous bars or cafes.

Pyrgos is a must-see location on every trip to Santorini, whether you're a history buff, an architecture enthusiast, or simply looking for a calm vacation. The rich history, breathtaking scenery, and lovely ambience of the village are guaranteed to make an indelible impression.

Megalochori: The Traditional Santorinian Village

Megalochori is a historic Santorinian village in the island's southwest, famed for its gorgeous architecture, attractive streets, and peaceful environment. Megalochori visitors can expect to be taken back in time, with centuries-old buildings and a sense of classic Greek culture.

History and Culture:
Megalochori has a long and fascinating history that dates back to the 17th century. The community is recognized for its unique architecture, which includes traditional cave houses, colorful structures, and small, meandering alleyways. Visitors can explore the village's several churches and chapels, including the famed 17th-century Agios Nikolaos Marmaritis.

Top Attractions:
In addition to historical and cultural sites, Megalochori is noted for its breathtaking views of the surrounding countryside and the Aegean Sea. Visitors can meander

through the village at their leisure, soaking in the magnificent views and sounds of this delightful old town.

Getting Around:
Megalochori is easily accessible from other sections of the island by bus or automobile. Visitors can also choose to walk around the village, soaking in the sights and sounds of this delightful old town.

Where to Stay:
Megalochori has a variety of lodging alternatives, including traditional guesthouses and luxurious villas. Visitors can stay in the town center, surrounded by attractive streets and buildings, or in the surrounding countryside, which offers a more calm and private ambiance.

Dining and Nightlife:
Megalochori has a variety of dining options, ranging from traditional tavernas providing traditional Greek cuisine to upmarket restaurants serving foreign cuisine. Visitors can also enjoy a drink or two at one of the village's numerous bars or cafes.

Megalochori is a must-see sight on every trip to Santorini, whether you're a history buff, an architecture lover, or simply looking for a calm vacation. The rich history, breathtaking scenery, and lovely ambience of the village are guaranteed to make an indelible impression.

Emporio: The Authentic and Off-the-Beaten-Path Village

Emporio is a beautiful village in Santorini's southeast, recognized for its true Greek environment and off-the-beaten-path ambiance. This quaint town is a hidden gem that tourists wishing to explore the island's lesser-known locations should uncover.

History and Culture:
Emporio has a lengthy and fascinating history that dates back to the medieval period. Visitors can stroll through the village's winding lanes and alleyways, which are adorned with whitewashed cottages, historic churches, and ancient ruins. The town is particularly notable for its unusual fortified tower houses, which served as defense structures during wartime.

Top Attractions:
Aside from its rich history and culture, Emporio has a variety of things to offer visitors. The main plaza of the hamlet is a hive of activity, with traditional tavernas, cafes, and stores. Visitors can also visit the local beaches, trek to

the medieval castle ruins, or simply rest and soak in the relaxed ambiance of this delightful village.

Getting Around:

From other sections of the island, Emporio is easily accessible by vehicle or bus. Visitors can also choose to walk around the village, soaking in the sights and sounds of this traditional Greek town.

Where to Stay:

Emporio has a variety of lodging options, ranging from traditional guesthouses and flats to luxurious villas. Visitors can stay in the town center, surrounded by attractive streets and buildings, or in the surrounding countryside, which offers a more calm and private ambiance.

Dining and Nightlife:

There are a variety of dining options in Emporio, ranging from traditional tavernas serving local food to upmarket restaurants providing foreign delicacies. Visitors can also enjoy a drink or two at one of the village's numerous bars or cafes.

Emporio is a must-see destination on any trip to Santorini, whether you're hoping to discover the island's lesser-known destinations or simply seeking a laid-back retreat. The rich history, authentic Greek culture, and off-the-beaten-path surroundings of the village are guaranteed to leave an impact.

CHAPTER 3:
DISCOVERING SANTORINI'S
BEACHES

Santorini is famous for its breathtaking caldera views and medieval villages, but the island also has some of the most gorgeous beaches in the Aegean Sea. Santorini's beaches provide guests with a one-of-a-kind and spectacular experience, with a combination of black, red, and white sands, stunning cliffs, and crystal-clear waters.

In this chapter, we'll look at some of the island's top beaches, each with its distinct features and ambiance. There is a beach for every sort of traveler, from the popular and crowded Red Beach to the serene Vlychada Beach.

Santorini's beaches are not to be missed, whether you want to swim, sunbathe, or simply take in the spectacular views. So take your sunscreen and a towel, and let's go on a journey to discover Santorini's beautiful beaches.

Perissa and Perivolos: The Famous Black Sand Beaches

Perissa and Perivolos are two of Santorini's most famous beaches, famed for their distinctive black sand and crystal-clear waters. They are easily accessible from the cities of Fira and Oia, which are located on the island's southeastern coast.

Perissa Beach is a long expanse of black sand with an abundance of rental sun loungers and umbrellas. Along the waterfront, there are also various beach bars and restaurants, making it a perfect place to spend the day. If you want to spend a more active day at the beach, water sports such as jet skiing and windsurfing are available.

Perivolos Beach is another beautiful black sand beach located just south of Perissa. There are lots of beachfront amenities accessible, including sun loungers, umbrellas, and beach bars, just like in Perissa. Perivolos, on the other hand, is recognized for its more laid-back and calm environment, making it an excellent choice for those seeking a quieter day at the beach.

Perissa and Perivolos are both excellent choices for families, couples, or lone visitors wishing to spend a day basking in the sun and swimming in the pristine waters of the Aegean Sea.

Kamari: The Lively Beach with Crystal-Clear Waters

Kamari is a bustling beach on Santorini's eastern coast. Kamari is a popular destination for people wishing to enjoy the sun and sea. It is known for its crystal-clear seas and a lengthy stretch of black sand.

Sun loungers, umbrellas, and beach bars are among the many amenities accessible at Kamari. Water sports such as kayaking, paddle boarding, and snorkeling are also available at the beach. There are various diving centers in the region if you want to explore the underwater world.

Kamari also has a bustling promenade dotted with restaurants, cafes, and stores selling everything from souvenirs to beachwear. There are numerous dining alternatives, ranging from traditional Greek cuisine to foreign fare.

There are other surrounding places worth seeing if you want to get away from the beach, such as the historic city of Thera and the Monastery of Prophet Elias. Kamari is also well-connected to the rest of the island, with buses traveling to Fira and other towns regularly.

Kamari has something for everyone, whether you're searching for a day of rest or adventure.

Red Beach: The Dramatic and Colorful Beach

Red Beach is one of Santorini's most stunning and colorful beaches. The beach is recognized for its dramatic red and black volcanic sand, which contrasts nicely with the Aegean Sea's crystal-clear waters.

Red Beach, near the municipality of Akrotiri, is flanked by cliffs and rock formations, making it a favorite destination for photographers and nature enthusiasts. The beach is modest, but there is plenty of space to spread out a towel and soak up the rays.

Swimming at Red Beach is a one-of-a-kind experience because the water is shallow and can be fairly warm. The beach is also ideal for snorkeling, with a plethora of colorful fish and underwater tunnels to discover.

While there are no facilities on the beach, there are a number of tavernas and cafes nearby that provide traditional Greek cuisine and cool drinks. A short trek up to the ruins of Akrotiri, an ancient Minoan settlement buried by a volcanic eruption in the 17th century BC, is equally worthwhile.

Overall, Red Beach is a must-see for anybody visiting Santorini, providing a breathtaking natural landscape and a one-of-a-kind beach experience.

Vlychada: The Secluded Beach with Unforgettable Scenery

Vlychada is a secluded beach on Santorini's southern shore recognized for its beautiful views and lunar-like environment. The beach is flanked by high white cliffs that have been sculpted over thousands of years by the wind and seas, producing a magnificent and otherworldly sight.

The beach is very calm and secluded, making it ideal for people looking to get away from the crowds and spend some time relaxing by the sea. The sand is a mix of black and gray, and the water is clean and tranquil, making it an ideal location for swimming and sunbathing.

Vlychada also has some of the most popular beach bars and restaurants on the island, which serve wonderful food and refreshing drinks in a pleasant and laid-back setting. There are also several chances for water sports and activities like kayaking and paddleboarding.

Exploring the neighboring marina, which is home to dozens of traditional fishing boats and yachts, is one of the attractions of a visit to Vlychada. The marina is an excellent location for photography and provides insight into the island's traditional way of life.

Overall, Vlychada is a must-see for anyone wishing to immerse themselves in the natural beauty and peacefulness of Santorini's shore, with stunning scenery and a relaxing and peaceful attitude.

Koloumbo: The Hidden and Unspoiled Beach

Koloumbo Beach is a hidden treasure on Santorini's northeastern coast. Unlike the island's more popular beaches, Koloumbo Beach has remained undisturbed by heavy tourism, making it a great place for those seeking a hidden and peaceful escape.

The beach is located at the base of a high cliff, which makes for a magnificent backdrop for swimming and sunbathing. The sand is a mix of black and gray, and the water is clear, making it an ideal location for snorkeling and exploring the undersea world.

The hike down to the beach is one of the joys of visiting Koloumbo Beach. The walk to the beach is steep and rocky, but the spectacular vistas and natural beauty along the way make it well worth the effort.

Koloumbo Beach has no beach facilities or restaurants, therefore visitors should carry their food and water. The absence of services, on the other hand, adds to the beach's quiet and unspoiled ambiance, making it a one-of-a-kind and remarkable spot to visit.

Overall, Koloumbo Beach is a must-see for anyone wishing to get away from the throng and enjoy the natural beauty and solitude of Santorini's shoreline.

CHAPTER 4:

UNCOVERING SANTORINI'S

HISTORY AND CULTURE

Santorini is a one-of-a-kind destination known not only for its breathtaking natural beauty but also for its rich and fascinating history and culture. The island has a rich and diverse cultural past that awaits exploration, ranging from ancient civilizations to modern-day traditions.

In this chapter, we'll delve into Santorini's history and culture, taking a closer look at the island's past and present. We will look at the ancient civilizations that formerly occupied the island, such as the Minoans, Greeks, and Romans, and how they influenced Santorini's culture and architecture.

We'll also look at the island's recent history, such as its role in the Greek War of Independence and its transformation into a major tourist destination. We will discover the unique arts and crafts that are still created on the island today, as well as the historic architecture and local customs that have been preserved over the ages.

This chapter will provide a detailed overview of Santorini's unique history and culture and will help you develop a better appreciation and understanding of this gorgeous destination, whether you are a history buff, a cultural enthusiast, or simply inquisitive about the island's past and present.

The Minoan Civilization: Exploring Akrotiri's Archaeological Site

The Minoan Civilization was one of the world's most advanced ancient civilizations, and its repercussions may still be seen in modern-day Greece. Santorini played an important role in Minoan history, and nowhere is this more clear than at the Akrotiri Archaeological Site.

Akrotiri, located on the island's southern tip, was a thriving Minoan settlement that was destroyed by a huge volcanic eruption in the 17th century BC. The ash from the eruption, one of the greatest in recorded history, covered the entire settlement and preserved it for thousands of years.

Today, visitors can explore the surprisingly well-preserved ruins of Akrotiri, which offer an intriguing view into Minoan daily life and culture. The site has magnificent constructions like multi-story buildings, paved streets, and extensive drainage systems, as well as beautiful frescoes and artifacts that demonstrate the Minoans' outstanding artistic and technological abilities.

You'll be transported back in time as you explore the site, to a world that existed thousands of years ago. You'll be astounded by the brilliant urban design and engineering that allowed the Minoans to exist in such a harsh climate, and you'll gain a better grasp of the impact the volcanic eruption had on their civilization.

Anyone interested in ancient history and archaeology should go to the Akrotiri Archaeological Site. Santorini is a location that has something for everyone, thanks to its interesting history and magnificent natural beauty.

The Bronze Age Eruption: How Santorini's Landscape Was Formed

Santorini's distinct and attractive scenery did not always exist as it does now. Indeed, the island's current shape and beauty are the result of a devastating event that occurred almost 3,500 years ago. This was a volcanic eruption that destroyed the Minoan civilisation on the island of Thera and resulted in one of the greatest volcanic explosions ever recorded in human history.

The Bronze Age eruption, which took place approximately 1600 BCE, was a devastating event that not only devastated the Minoan civilisation but also changed the entire Aegean region. The eruption was so powerful that it blasted an estimated 60 cubic kilometers of volcanic material into the atmosphere, resulting in the formation of a caldera that can still be seen today.

The eruption left an ash and pumice covering that blanketed the island, protecting its buildings and treasures. These relics are today a treasure trove for archaeologists, historians, and interested visitors seeking to comprehend

71

the events that molded Santorini and the surrounding region.

Visitors to Santorini can learn about the Bronze Age eruption and its influence on the island by visiting the archaeological site of Akrotiri, which has revealed the remnants of an ancient Minoan city. The site offers an exceptional insight into Minoan life and the disastrous events that led to their downfall.

The Bronze Age eruption also left an indelible mark on Santorini's culture and identity. Today, the island is famed for its distinctive architecture, cuisine, and wine, all of which reflect the volcanic scenery and the island's rich past. Santorini visitors can learn about the island's history and culture by visiting museums, vineyards, and traditional villages where the legacy of the Bronze Age eruption can still be found.

The Byzantine Era: Discovering Santorini's Medieval History

The Byzantine era had a huge impact on the history of Santorini, and remnants of this time may still be found around the island today. Following the demise of the Roman Empire, the Byzantine Empire dominated the Mediterranean. Santorini was a part of this empire, and its strategic location made it an important trading and economic center.

The island underwent a great cultural and artistic rebirth during this time. Many Byzantine churches and monasteries were built, and their unique architecture and art still beautify the landscape of the island. One of the most well-known examples is Mesa Gonia's Church of Panagia Episkopi, which was established in the 11th century and is one of the island's oldest churches.

Santorini's Byzantine history ended in 1204 when the island was taken by the Venetians during the Fourth Crusade.

The Venetian Rule: Exploring Santorini's Renaissance Architecture

Santorini was conquered by the Venetians in the 13th century and became a part of the Venetian Republic. This period of Venetian sovereignty lasted over 300 years and had a lasting impact on the architecture and culture of the island.

The Venetians brought a new architectural style to Santorini, with Renaissance elements such as arched windows and doors, ornamental balconies, and elaborate façade. During this time, several of the island's churches and houses were built, notably the famed Santozeum Museum in Fira, which was previously the residence of a wealthy Venetian family.

Aside from building, the Venetians had a huge impact on Santorini's culture and economy. They built a booming wine industry on the island and many of the vineyards and wineries that still exist today date from this period.

Exploring the legacy of Venetian control is a must-do during any visit to Santorini, as it provides visitors with an insight into the island's rich and diverse history.

The Modern Era: Santorini's Cultural Renaissance and Revival

Santorini's modern age began in the mid-twentieth century, when tourism began to flourish, bringing with it a renewed interest in the island's culture and history. Santorini is currently known not only for its breathtaking natural beauty, but also for its thriving cultural life.

The Santorini Arts plant, built in an old tomato canning plant in Vlychada, is one of the most important cultural events on the island. Cultural events at the factory include theatrical performances, art exhibitions, concerts, and dance acts.

The local wine industry is also a key part of Santorini's cultural rebirth. The volcanic soil and unusual climate of the island make it a perfect place for grape cultivation, and Santorini is now known for producing some of the world's most exceptional wines. Visitors can tour the wineries on the island, learn about the winemaking process, and sample some of the great local wines.

Santorini boasts various museums that reflect the island's history and legacy, in addition to these cultural attractions. The Archaeological Museum of Thera in Fira displays Minoan relics, whilst the Museum of Prehistoric Thera in Akrotiri depicts the ancient city buried by the volcanic disaster.

Santorini has plenty to offer any traveler, whether they are interested in art, wine, history, or simply soaking up the local culture.

CHAPTER 5:
SAVORING SANTORINI'S CUISINE AND WINE

Welcome to Santorini's gastronomic journey, where the island's rich history and unique geography have produced an exceptional culinary scene. Santorini is home to some of the world's most magnificent fruits, from juicy cherry tomatoes and tangy white eggplants to delicious capers and fava beans, thanks to its volcanic soil and ample sunshine.

In this chapter, we will delve into the island's rich culinary legacy, beginning with traditional dishes passed down through generations. Then we'll move on to contemporary cuisine, where creative chefs combine classic ingredients with cutting-edge techniques. Of course, Santorini's world-renowned wines, including crisp whites and strong reds, must be included.

So prepare your taste buds for a gourmet adventure around Santorini, one of Greece's most exquisite islands.

Traditional Tavernas: Where to Taste Authentic Santorinian Dishes

Santorini's cuisine is a fusion of traditional Greek and Mediterranean flavors, resulting in a one-of-a-kind and delectable gourmet experience. The greatest places to try real Santorinian food cooked with fresh, locally produced ingredients are traditional tavernas. These family-run enterprises provide a quiet and private atmosphere in which to enjoy a meal while feeling like a member of the local community.

Fava, a yellow split pea puree topped with onions and capers; tomato fritters, fried balls made from Santorini's famous cherry tomatoes; and moussaka, a layered eggplant and pork casserole topped with creamy béchamel sauce, are among the must-try meals. Grilled octopus and squid are popular seafood options, while spicy meatballs cooked with cumin and garlic are popular among meat eaters.

When dining in a taverna, be sure to order a glass of local wine to go with your meal. The volcanic soil and Mediterranean temperature of Santorini make it a perfect location for wine growing, and the island's wineries produce some of Greece's best wines. The most well-known grape variety farmed on the island is Assyrtiko, which comes in both white and red variants. Nykteri, Vinsanto, and Athiri are also prominent wine varieties.

Upscale Restaurants: Where to Enjoy Fine Dining with a View

Santorini's cuisine is not only flavorful and aromatic but also visually appealing, providing a whole gastronomic experience. Santorini offers numerous luxury restaurants to select from if you're seeking a fine dining experience with an incredible view.

Selene, a Michelin-starred restaurant in Fira, serves inventive Greek food with a modern twist. Their recipes are made with locally obtained ingredients and display the traditional flavors of the island uniquely. Selene is a wonderful gastronomic delight, with a panoramic view of the caldera.

Lauda, located in Oia, is another noteworthy restaurant. Lauda is a Mediterranean restaurant that serves a tasting menu with fresh seafood and local ingredients. The restaurant's terrace overlooks the sea and provides a spectacular view of the sunset.

Armeni, situated in Oia, is another restaurant with a spectacular view of the caldera. Their menu focuses on Mediterranean cuisine with an emphasis on seafood, and their wine list includes some of the greatest Santorini and Greek wines.

Lycabettus in Fira has a more casual vibe. The restaurant has a terrace with a spectacular view of the caldera and serves traditional Greek cuisine created with fresh island ingredients.

Whatever restaurant you select, Santorini's luxury restaurants provide a spectacular gastronomic experience while providing incomparable views of the island's natural beauty.

Wineries: Where to Taste Santorini's Distinctive Wines

Santorini is well-known for its distinctive wines, which are made from grapes grown in the volcanic soil of the island. Visiting a winery during your trip to Santorini is a must-do experience since you'll get to try some of the island's distinctive wines and learn about the wine-making process.

On the island, there are various wineries, each with its own distinct experience. Santo Wines, which enjoys beautiful views of the caldera, and Venetsanos Winery, which is nestled into the cliffs and offers panoramic views of the sea, are two of the most popular vineyards.

You'll be able to try a variety of wines at each winery, including Assyrtiko, the island's distinctive white wine.

You'll also have the opportunity to learn about the wine-making process and the peculiar growing conditions that distinguish Santorini's wines.

Many vineyards also provide food pairings, so you may sample traditional Santorinian delicacies while sipping your wine.

Visiting a winery is a must-do activity during your trip to Santorini, whether you're a wine lover or simply searching for a unique experience.

CHAPTER 6:
SHOPPING AND NIGHTLIFE IN SANTORINI

Santorini is more than just a vacation spot for sun, sand, and sea. It's also a great area to go shopping and check out the busy nightlife scene. The island has a varied shopping and entertainment environment to suit every taste and budget.

Santorini has it all, from boutique shops selling handmade goods and jewelry to stylish bars serving distinctive cocktails. This chapter is dedicated to assisting visitors in discovering the greatest shops and nightlife on the island.

Santorini has something for everyone, whether you're seeking unique souvenirs, high-end clothes, or a night out on the town. So take your cash and your dancing shoes, and let's explore Santorini's shopping and nightlife scene.

Local Products: What to Try and Where to Buy

The volcanic soil and unique climate of Santorini provide a fertile ground for generating remarkable indigenous items that are not found anyplace else in the world. Here are a few must-try local products to try during your stay in Santorini:

Santorini's Cherry Tomatoes: The volcanic soil and abundant sunshine give Santorini's cherry tomatoes a distinct, rich flavor. They are available in traditional taverns, marketplaces, and grocery stores.

Fava: Fava is a golden split-pea purée that is popular in Santorini cuisine. It is great with grilled fish or meat as a dip or as a side dish.

White Eggplant: Santorini's white eggplant is a distinct kind with a little sweeter flavor than regular eggplants. It is typically grilled, roasted, or fried.

Capers: Santorini's capers are small, delicate, and flavorful. Salads, sauces, and seafood meals all contain them.

Wine: The volcanic soil and climate of Santorini form a distinct terroir that produces superb wines. The major grape varietals used to make Santorini's characteristic white wines are Assyrtiko, Athiri, and Aidani. You can sample and learn about the wine-making process by visiting some of the island's wineries.

These items can be found at local markets, grocery stores, and specialized shops throughout the island. Make sure to sample them on your visit to Santorini and bring some home as souvenirs.

Best Souvenirs to Buy in Santorini

Santorini is well-known for its wonderful handcrafted crafts and local products, making it an excellent place for souvenir shopping. Here are some of the best Santorini souvenirs to buy:

Ceramics: Santorini's volcanic soil and natural clay deposits make it a mecca for handcrafted ceramics. Vases, plates, bowls, and decorative objects with traditional designs can be found among the ceramic goods.

Local Wines: The volcanic soil and dry environment of Santorini have resulted in the creation of some of Greece's finest wines. Assyrtiko, Athiri, and Aidani are the most popular types. You can go wine tasting at local wineries and buy bottles to take home.

Jewelry: Santorini's indigenous jewelers produce one-of-a-kind items inspired by the island's history and culture. Beautiful objects fashioned with precious stones, pearls, and gold that represent the beauty of the island can be found.

Olive Oil & Herbs: Some of Greece's best olive trees and herb gardens may be found on Santorini. Bottles of locally made olive oil, oregano, and other herbs can be purchased to lend a unique flavor to your food.

Honey: The wildflowers and thyme bushes of Santorini create an ideal setting for honeybees. The honey from the island is noted for its great taste and quality.

Handmade Textiles: The textile business in Santorini is well-known for its unique designs and high-quality materials. Handmade scarves, shawls, and purses made of silk, cotton, and wool are available.

Local Sweets: Santorini's sweet delicacies come in a variety of tastes, including pistachio, almond, and honey. These sweets are available at local bakeries and sweet shops.

Before making a purchase, remember to shop around and check prices. Many shops and stalls sell comparable products, so take your time and choose the right souvenir to take home with you.

Shopping Areas

Santorini's various little shops and boutiques dispersed throughout the island provide a one-of-a-kind shopping experience. Here are some of the top shopping districts to visit:

Fira: Santorini's busy city is the shopping mecca, with a wide range of businesses selling anything from souvenirs to designer clothes and jewelry.

Oia: Another famous shopping destination is the picturesque village on the caldera's edge, which is famed for its art galleries, souvenir shops, and high-end boutiques.

Kamari: This seaside resort town is ideal for shopping for beachwear, accessories, and local handicrafts.

Emporio: A variety of stores sell handcrafted pottery, jewelry, and other locally manufactured products in the traditional village.

Pyrgos: This scenic hilltop village is ideal for shopping for traditional products such as honey, olive oil, and wine.

Akrotiri: There is a tiny shop on the archaeological site that sells local products and souvenirs.

No matter where you travel in Santorini, you'll find lots of possibilities for shopping and exploring the island's distinctive items.

Best Bars and Clubs in Santorini

Santorini is famous for its active nightlife as well as its beautiful scenery, unique cuisine, and rich culture. The island has something for everyone, whether you want to dance the night away or enjoy a drink with a view. Here are some of the greatest Santorini pubs and clubs:

Koo Club - Koo Club, located in Fira, is a popular destination for those searching for a great night out. Koo Club is a must-see for partygoers due to its lively environment, amazing music, and wide dance floor.

Tango Bar - Located in Oia, this bar offers amazing views of the caldera. Tango Bar is ideal for people looking for a drink while viewing the sunset or a romantic night out.

Murphy's Bar - Murphy's Bar, located in Perissa, is popular with both locals and tourists. This laid-back bar with live music is a fantastic place to unwind after a day of visiting the island.

Enigma Club - Located in Fira, Enigma Club is one of the island's largest clubs. Enigma Club is the place to be for electronic music fans, with its futuristic design, cutting-edge sound system, and world-class DJs.

Two Brothers Bar - Two Brothers Bar is a family-owned establishment in Kamari that offers a welcoming atmosphere with live music. This pub is ideal for individuals who wish to unwind with a drink in a relaxing setting.

Franco's Bar - Franco's Bar in Fira is famous for its panoramic views of the caldera. This bar is ideal for individuals who wish to sip a cocktail while admiring the scenery.

Tropical Bar - Tropical Bar, located in Perissa, is a popular destination for those looking for a beach bar experience. Tropical Bar is a must-visit for those looking to soak up the sun and have some fun, with its sandy beachfront location, delicious cocktails, and live music.

These bars and clubs are sure to give you an outstanding experience.

Festivals & Events

Santorini is renowned not just for its breathtaking vistas, but also for its dynamic cultural scene, which hosts several events and festivals throughout the year. Here are a few of the most popular:

The Santorini Arts Factory is a cultural facility that conducts a variety of events, such as art exhibitions, music concerts, and theatrical plays.

Ifestia celebration: This celebration, held in late September, honors the volcanic eruption that built Santorini. It includes pyrotechnics, live music, and an eruption reenactment.

Santorini Jazz Event: This event, held in early September, features local and international jazz musicians.

Santorini Experience: This athletic event, held in October, features swimming and running races throughout the island.

Wine Festivals: Santorini is known for its distinctive wines, and many wine festivals are held throughout the year, including the Santorini Wine Festival in August and the Santorini Wine Roads Festival in November.

Easter Celebrations: Easter is a Christian holiday in Greece, and Santorini has several distinctive traditions, such as the burning of Judas' effigies on Good Friday and the Easter Saturday fireworks display.

Summer Music Festivals: Many music festivals are held in Santorini during the summer months, with local and worldwide performers performing in a range of genres.

Traditional Festivals: Throughout the year, various traditional festivals commemorate religious and cultural events. The Feast of St. John the Baptist in June is one of the most popular, with feasting, music, and dancing.

These events and festivals contribute to Santorini's cultural richness and give tourists one-of-a-kind experiences and memories.

CHAPTER 7:

7-DAY ITINERARY IN SANTORINI

Day 1: Arrival and Sunset in Oia

Morning:

Arrive at Santorini in the morning and check into your accommodations. After your journey, take some time to rest and refresh.

Afternoon:

Visit Oia, one of the most renowned and gorgeous sites on the island. Explore the small alleyways adorned with white-washed buildings and blue-domed churches, and see the caldera vistas. The Oia Castle provides some of the best sunset views on the island.

Evening:

From Oia, watch the beautiful Santorini sunset. Enjoy a drink or a meal at one of the caldera's many eateries or pubs.

Accommodation:

Stay at Oia or a nearby village for easy access to the village and its sunset views.

Note: Please keep in mind that depending on when you arrive, you may have more or less time to explore Oia on your first day.

Day 2: Exploring the Caldera and Fira

Morning:

Get up early to see the spectacular sunrise over the Caldera. One of the most popular viewpoints on the island is Oia Castle. Explore the lovely alleys and whitewashed buildings of Oia after viewing the sunrise. Take a walk down the main street, appreciating the one-of-a-kind boutiques and shops along the route. Stop in one of the many cafes overlooking the Caldera for a coffee or a quick breakfast.

Afternoon:

In the afternoon, go to Fira, Santorini's capital. Take the cable car or the steps down to the old port, where you may board a catamaran for a tour of the Caldera. Explore the volcanic islands and cool yourself in the hot springs. Along the route, marvel at the unusual rock formations and vibrant coastlines.

Evening:
Return to Fira in the evening to enjoy the busy nightlife. Begin with a cocktail at one of the many bars with views of the Caldera. Then, for dinner, visit one of the town's classic tavernas. Santorini's famed delicacies include fava, tomato fritters, and white eggplant. Finish the night by strolling through the town's alleyways, delighting in the frenetic atmosphere and illuminated structures.

Accommodation:
Depending on your preferences, spend the night in Fira or Oia. Fira has a broader selection of lodging alternatives, ranging from luxury hotels to budget-friendly hostels. With many boutique hotels and villas overlooking the Caldera, Oia has a more upmarket ambiance.

Day 3: Exploring Santorini's Beaches

Morning: Perissa and Perivolos Beaches

Begin your day by visiting the famous black sand beaches of Perissa and Perivolos, which are located on the island's southeastern shore. Swim in the crystal-clear seas, sunbathe on the black sand, and explore the area in the morning. There are numerous beachside pubs and restaurants where you may have a cool drink or a bite to eat.

Afternoon: Kamari Beach

In the afternoon, head to Kamari Beach, which is located just north of Perissa and Perivolos. This bustling beach is well-known for its long stretch of pebbly shore and lovely seas. Rent a sunbed and an umbrella and relax by the sea, or participate in water sports like paddleboarding, kayaking, or jet skiing.

Evening: Dinner in Fira

Return to Fira as the sun begins to set for a great meal at one of the town's many eateries. Traditional Santorinian foods like fava, tomato fritters, and moussaka go well with a drink of local wine. After supper, meander around Fira's lovely neighborhoods and take in the views of the caldera illuminated at night.

Accommodation: For convenient access to the island's beaches and nightlife, stay in Fira or Kamari.

Day 4: Exploring the Villages of Santorini

Morning: Pyrgos Village
Begin your day by visiting Pyrgos, a lovely hilltop village in Santorini's heart. Take a walk through the narrow streets and observe the traditional Cycladic architecture. For panoramic views of the island, visit the Venetian castle at the top of the settlement.

Afternoon: Megalochori Village
Then, continue to Megalochori, another picturesque Santorinian village that has kept its ancient character. Take a stroll around the small streets, admiring the white-washed buildings and blue-domed churches. Stop at one of the local tavernas for a classic Greek lunch.

Evening: Sunset in Oia

No journey to Santorini is complete unless you see the iconic sunset in Oia. Find a vantage point on the island's northern edge to watch the sun slowly sink into the Aegean Sea. After that, take a stroll through Oia's charming streets and indulge in some shopping or dinner at one of the many eateries.

Accommodation:

Spend the night in Oia to appreciate the atmosphere and avoid traveling back to your accommodation in the dark.

Day 5: Caldera Cruise and Sunset in Oia

Morning:

Begin your day with an exhilarating Caldera cruise, which brings you to some of Santorini's most beautiful sites. Depending on your preferences, you can book a half-day or full-day cruise. You have the option of taking a small group tour or a personalized tour. Most trips include stops at the Palea Kameni hot springs, Thirassia island, and a dip at Red Beach.

Afternoon:

After the boat, return to Fira and eat lunch at one of the local tavernas. Traditional Greek foods such as moussaka, souvlaki, and fresh seafood are available.

Evening:

In the evening, head to Oia to see the beautiful sunset. Oia is famous for its breathtaking caldera views and lovely white and blue buildings. You can walk around town and shop before finding a spot to watch the sunset. The sunset in Oia is a must-see, so arrive early to ensure a decent place.

Accommodation:

Depending on your preferences, spend the night in Oia or Fira. Both towns have a wide range of lodging alternatives to suit your budget and needs.

Day 6: Day at the Beach and Wine Tasting

Morning:

After a few days of sightseeing, take a more leisurely approach to the day by visiting one of Santorini's lovely beaches. Perissa and Kamari are two of the most popular destinations, with black sand beaches and crystal-clear waters. Relax on the beach, swim in the Aegean Sea, and enjoy the sunshine.

Afternoon:

After a morning of beach activities, spend the afternoon wine tasting at one of Santorini's famed wineries. The volcanic soil and climate of the island create some of the world's most distinct and exquisite wines. You can have a guided tour and wine tasting at one of the region's many vineyards, such as Santo Wines or Venetsanos Winery.

Evening:

Finish the day with a great dinner at one of the many restaurants on the island. Traditional Greek cuisine is available, as is a more modern take on Mediterranean dishes. Metaxi Mas in Exo Gonia and Selene in Pyrgos are two popular choices.

Accommodation:
To prevent a long trip back to your accommodation after wine tasting, stay in the same area as your chosen winery. Alternatively, you can stay near the beach and spend the night at Perissa or Kamari.

Day 7: Departure Day

Morning: Last-minute shopping
Take some time before you leave Santorini to shop for souvenirs and gifts for your loved ones. Many businesses in Fira and Oia sell local handicrafts such as handmade ceramics, jewelry, and textiles. You can also go to a local market and stock up on great Greek food to take home.

Afternoon: Departure
Check out of your accommodation and make your way to the airport or port of departure. You may have time for one last lunch in Santorini, depending on your departure time.

Try a classic Greek breakfast or brunch at one of the nearby cafés.

This itinerary is only a sample and can be tailored to your preferences and interests. Have a pleasant and safe journey!

CHAPTER 8:
PRACTICAL INFORMATION AND
TIPS

Customs and Etiquette

Customs and etiquette are essential parts of any culture, including Santorini. To guarantee a successful and polite stay, visitors to the island should be informed of the local customs. Here are some recommendations for customs and etiquette for Santorini:

Dress Code: Although Santorini is a laid-back island, it is vital to dress appropriately when visiting churches or monasteries. When visiting religious locations, women should avoid wearing shorts and sleeveless shirts, and both men and women should cover their shoulders and knees. Bathing suits are only permitted on the beach and in the pool sections.

Greetings: Greeks are famed for their warmth and hospitality. People are typically greeted with a handshake and, in some situations, a kiss on both cheeks. Unless they allow you to address them by their first name, use formal titles such as "Mr." or "Mrs."

Tipping: Tipping is popular in Santorini, particularly at restaurants and cafes. A 10% tip is a good rule of thumb, but it depends on the level of service you received. Tipping tour guides, taxi drivers, and hotel employees are also customary.

Language: Santorini's official language is Greek, but English is commonly used, particularly in tourist areas. It's always a good idea to know a few Greek phrases like "hello" (yassou), "thank you" (efharisto), and "please" (parakalo).

Smoking: Santorini allows smoking in specific areas, however, it is becoming increasingly restricted. It's critical to obey the signs and avoid smoking in public places or restaurants unless it's explicitly permitted.

Respectful Behavior: Respect is valued in Greek culture, and visitors should be mindful of their behavior to avoid offending Greeks. Avoid noisy and disruptive behavior in public places, and observe local norms such as taking off your shoes before entering someone's home.

Tourists can guarantee a comfortable and polite stay in Santorini by following these easy suggestions and leaving a great impression on the locals.

Simple Language Phrases to Know

Santorini is a widely known tourist destination, hence English is commonly spoken, particularly in the main tourist areas. Learning a few simple Greek phrases, on the other hand, can enrich your trip and make interactions with locals more enjoyable. Here are some basic language phrases to learn:

Greeting:

Hello: Γειά σου (yia sou)

Goodbye: Αντίο (adio)

Good morning: Καλημέρα (kalimera)

Good evening: Καλησπέρα (kalispera)

Basic Phrases:

Please: Παρακαλώ (parakalo)

Thank you: Ευχαριστώ (efharisto)

Sorry: Συγνώμη (signomi)

Yes: Ναι (ne)

No: Όχι (ochi)

Excuse me: Συγγνώμη (signomi)

Restaurant Phrases:

Do you have a table available? : Έχετε διαθέσιμο τραπέζι; (echete diathesimo trapezi?)

What do you recommend? : Τι μας προτείνετε; (ti mas proteinete?)

The check, please: Το λογαριασμό, παρακαλώ (to logariasmo, parakalo)

Transportation Phrases:

How much does it cost? : Πόσο κοστίζει; (poso kostizi?)

Where is the bus stop? : Πού είναι η στάση του λεωφορείου; (pou ine i stasi tou leoforeiou?)

Can you take me to _____? : Μπορείτε να με πάτε στο _____; (borite na me pate sto _____?)

Shopping Phrases:

How much does it cost? : Πόσο κοστίζει; (poso kostizi?)

Can you give me a discount? : Μπορείτε να μου κάνετε έκπτωση; (borite na mou kanete ekptosi?)

Do you accept credit cards? : Δέχεστε πιστωτικές κάρτες; (dehete pistotikes kartes?)

These phrases will come in helpful when visiting Santorini, and the people will appreciate your effort to communicate in their language.

Health and Safety Tips

Santorini is generally a safe destination, but as with any other place, it's crucial to take precautions to guarantee your health and safety while traveling. Here are some tips to remember:

Sun Protection: Because Santorini is known for its hot and sunny weather, it is critical to wear sunscreen. Wear a hat, sunglasses, and SPF-rated sunscreen. Avoid being outside during the hottest portion of the day (between 12 and 3 p.m.).

Stay Hydrated: Staying hydrated in the heat requires drinking plenty of water. Carry a refillable water bottle with you and drink plenty of water throughout the day.

Watch Your Step: Because some of Santorini's streets are steep and uneven, it's crucial to wear comfortable shoes and exercise caution when walking.

Swimming Caution: Although the beaches in Santorini are stunning, some of them might have strong currents. Always swim in areas where there are lifeguards and heed any warnings.

Keep a check on Your stuff: While Santorini is generally a safe place, it's still a good idea to keep a check on your stuff, especially in crowded areas. Keep your stuff safe and avoid pickpockets.

Follow COVID-19 Guidelines: Wear a mask indoors and in crowded outdoor locations, practice social distancing, and wash your hands frequently, according to COVID-19 standards.

By following these tips, you can ensure a safe and pleasurable trip to Santorini.

Emergency Contacts

In the event of an emergency in Santorini, dial the following numbers:

Police: 100
Ambulance: 166
Fire department: 199
European emergency number: 112

It's worth noting that English is frequently spoken in Santorini, so you should be able to converse with emergency personnel. If you have a medical emergency, you can also go to the Santorini Health Center in Fira, which is open 24 hours a day, seven days a week.

Communication and Internet Access

Communication and internet access are required to keep connected when visiting Santorini. Here are some pointers and resources to help you stay connected when traveling:

Mobile Data: Santorini has excellent mobile data coverage, and most major mobile operators provide roaming services. A local SIM card can be purchased at the airport or in one of Santorini's mobile phone shops. This will provide you with high internet speeds as well as low costs for local and international calls.

Wi-Fi: The majority of hotels, cafes, and restaurants in Santorini provide free Wi-Fi to their customers. There are also public Wi-Fi hotspots in various regions, including as Fira and Oia. However, signal strength and speed may vary, so having a backup plan is recommended.

Internet Cafes: There are various internet cafes in Santorini where you can pay to use a computer and connect to the internet. Some of these establishments also provide printing and scanning services.

Messaging Apps: Popular messaging programs like WhatsApp, Viber, and Skype can be used to stay in touch with family and friends back home. These apps transmit messages, make audio or video conversations, and share photographs and videos using Wi-Fi or mobile data.

Useful Apps, Websites, and Maps

There are several applications, websites, and maps that can assist you in planning and navigating your vacation to Santorini. Here are some suggestions:

Google Maps: This is an app that every traveler should have. You may use it to locate your way around the island, get directions, and even look for nearby restaurants, stores, and attractions.

Visit Santorini: This is the tourism board's official webpage. It has a plethora of information about what to see and do on the island, as well as useful travel tips and guidance.

Santorini Secrets: This website is a fantastic resource for discovering off-the-beaten-path sites on the island. It also includes a list of suggested hotels, restaurants, and bars.

Santorini Map: A thorough map of the island showing all of the key routes, cities, and attractions. It can be used to plan your itinerary and navigate about the island.

MyGreeceTravelBlog: This blog is run by a travel specialist who has visited Santorini many times. It provides expert suggestions and insider insights into things to see and do on the island, as well as practical travel guidance.

Windfinder: This app delivers real-time weather updates and wind forecasts for Santorini, which is very beneficial if you intend to participate in water sports or other outdoor activities.

Google Translate: If you don't know Greek, Google Translate can help you connect with locals and interpret signs and menus. It can translate text in real-time, allowing you to communicate with someone who speaks a different language.

These applications, websites, and maps can help you have a more enjoyable and stress-free trip to Santorini. Make sure to download them before you go so you can use them offline if necessary.

CONCLUSION

With its gorgeous views, stunning sunsets, and lovely villages, Santorini is an Aegean Sea jewel. This travel guide has offered a full itinerary for a 7-day vacation to Santorini, including the best places to see, dine, and explore. Santorini has something for everyone, whether you're a foodie, a history enthusiast, or simply seeking for some relaxation.

In addition to the schedule, this guide includes practical information and advice to assist you in organizing your trip, such as transportation, lodging, and etiquette. While Santorini is a popular tourist destination, it is crucial to remember to respect the local customs and culture.

When visiting Santorini, carry comfortable walking shoes, sunscreen, and a camera to record the breathtaking sights. When swimming in the Aegean Sea, it is also critical to be hydrated and vigilant.

Take the time to admire Santorini's beauty and immerse yourself in the local culture. Santorini is a place that will leave you wanting more, whether it's watching the sunset in

Oia, visiting the ancient ruins of Akrotiri, or indulging in some excellent Greek cuisine.

So pack your bags, grab your camera, and prepare for a once-in-a-lifetime journey to Santorini, Greece.

Overall, Santorini is a genuinely magical place that will provide you with lifelong memories. This travel guide is intended to assist you in making the most of your visit and experiencing the beauty and charm of this Greek island. I hope you have a wonderful time in Santorini and make memories to last a lifetime.

Printed in Great Britain
by Amazon

27213523R00069